For Celia

First published 1986 by Walker Books Ltd,
87 Vauxhall Walk, London SE11 5HJ

This edition produced 2000 for The Book People Ltd
Hall Wood Avenue, Haydock, St Helens WA11 9UL

2 4 6 8 10 9 7 5 3 1

© 1986 Shirley Hughes

This book has been typeset in Vendome.

Printed in Hong Kong

British Library Cataloguing in Publication Data
A catalogue record for this book is
available from the British Library.

ISBN 0-7445-6741-6

Colours

Shirley Hughes

TED SMART

blue

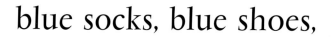

Baby blues,
navy blues,
blue socks, blue shoes,

Blue plate, blue mug,
blue flowers in a blue jug.

And fluffy white clouds floating by

In a great big beautiful bright blue sky.

yellow

Syrup dripping from a spoon,

Buttercups,

A harvest moon.

Sun like honey on the floor,

Warm as the steps by our back door.

red

Rosy apples, dark cherries,

Scarlet leaves, bright berries.

And when the winter's day is done,
A fiery sky, a big red sun.

Red and yellow make

orange

Tangerines and apricots,

Orange flowers in orange pots.

Orange glow on an orange mat,
Marmalade toast and a marmalade cat.

Blue and red make

purple

Berries in the bramble patch.

Pick them (but mind the

thorns don't scratch)!

Purple blossom, pale and dark,
Spreading with springtime in the park.

Blue and yellow make

green

Grasshoppers, greenflies,
gooseberries, cat's eyes.

Green lettuce, green peas,

Green shade from green trees.

And grass as far as you can see

Like green waves in a green sea.

black

Shiny boots,
A witch's hat.
Black cloak,
Black cat.

Black crows cawing high,
Winter trees against the sky.

white

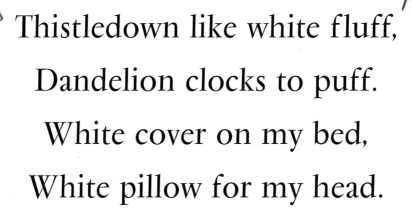

Thistledown like white fluff,

Dandelion clocks to puff.

White cover on my bed,

White pillow for my head.

White snowflakes, whirling down,
Covering gardens, roofs and towns.